Queen Alexandra's Birdwing

The World's Largest Butterfly

by John Stidworthy

Consultant: Jan Pasternak
Lepidopterist/Conservationist

BEARPORT
PUBLISHING

New York, New York

Credits

Cover, François Gilson/Peter Arnold; 2–3, ©Mike Howlett; 4, Kathrin Ayer; 4–5, ©Jan Pasternak; 6–7, ©Jan Pasternak; 8, ©Robert Gotts; 9BKG, ©Jan Pasternak; 10 (inset), ©Jan Pasternak; 10–11, ©Muriel Hazan/BIOS/Peter Arnold; 12–13, ©Jan Pasternak; 14, ©Mark Bowler/NHPA; 15, ©Jan Pasternak; 16–17, ©Jan Pasternak; 18 (inset), ©Jan Pasternak; 18–19, ©François Gilson/Peter Arnold; 20–21, ©François Gilson/BIOS/Peter Arnold; 22L, ©Barbara St. Madova/Photo Researchers; 22C, ©Ray Coleman/Photo Researchers; 22R, ©Stephen Dalton/NHPA; 23TL, ©Jan Pasternak; 23TR, Robert Gotts; 23BL, ©Joll Bricout/BIOS/Peter Arnold; 23BR, ©Friedrich Stark/Peter Arnold; 23BKG, ©Robert Gotts.

Publisher: Kenn Goin
Project Editor: Lisa Wiseman
Editorial Development: Nancy Hall, Inc.
Creative Director: Spencer Brinker
Photo Researcher: Carousel Research, Inc.: Mary Teresa Giancoli
Design: Otto Carbajal

Library of Congress Cataloging-in-Publication Data

Stidworthy, John, 1943-
    Queen Alexandra's birdwing : the world's largest butterfly / by John Stidworthy.
        p. cm. — (SuperSized!)
Includes bibliographical references and index.
ISBN-13: 978-1-59716-395-8 (library binding)
ISBN-10: 1-59716-395-3 (library binding)
1. Queen Alexandra's birdwing—Juvenile literature. I. Title.

QL561.P2S75 2007
595.78'9—dc22

                            2006036113

For more information, write to Bearport Publishing Company, Inc., 101 Fifth Avenue, Suite 6R, New York, New York 10003. Printed in the United States of America.

10 9 8 7 6 5 4 3 2 1

Contents

Wide Wings

The Queen Alexandra's birdwing is the largest butterfly in the world.

A female Queen Alexandra's birdwing is larger than the book you are reading.

A female Queen Alexandra's birdwing can be up to 12 inches (30 cm) long from wingtip to wingtip.

Male and Female Birdwings

Female Queen Alexandra's birdwings are bigger than males.

The female's wings are brown with cream and yellow markings.

Male birdwings are more colorful.

Their wings are blue, green, yellow, and black.

.

A male Queen Alexandra's birdwing is about 8 inches (20 cm) long from wingtip to wingtip.

A Forest Home

The Queen Alexandra's birdwing lives in **rain forests**.

It is found in just one tiny part of Papua New Guinea.

This butterfly was discovered by a scientist in 1906.

Queen Alexandra's Birdwings in the Wild

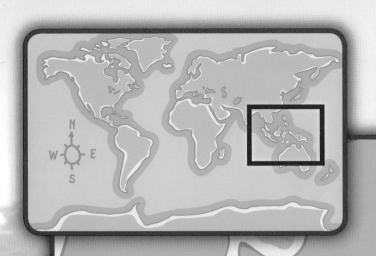

Pacific Ocean

Indian Ocean

Papua New Guinea

Australia

 Where Queen Alexandra's birdwings live

A Changing Life

The Queen Alexandra's birdwing goes through many changes before it becomes a butterfly.

It starts out as an egg.

A female birdwing lays the egg on a special plant called a **pipevine**.

The birdwing lives only in the parts of the forest where the pipevine grows.

egg

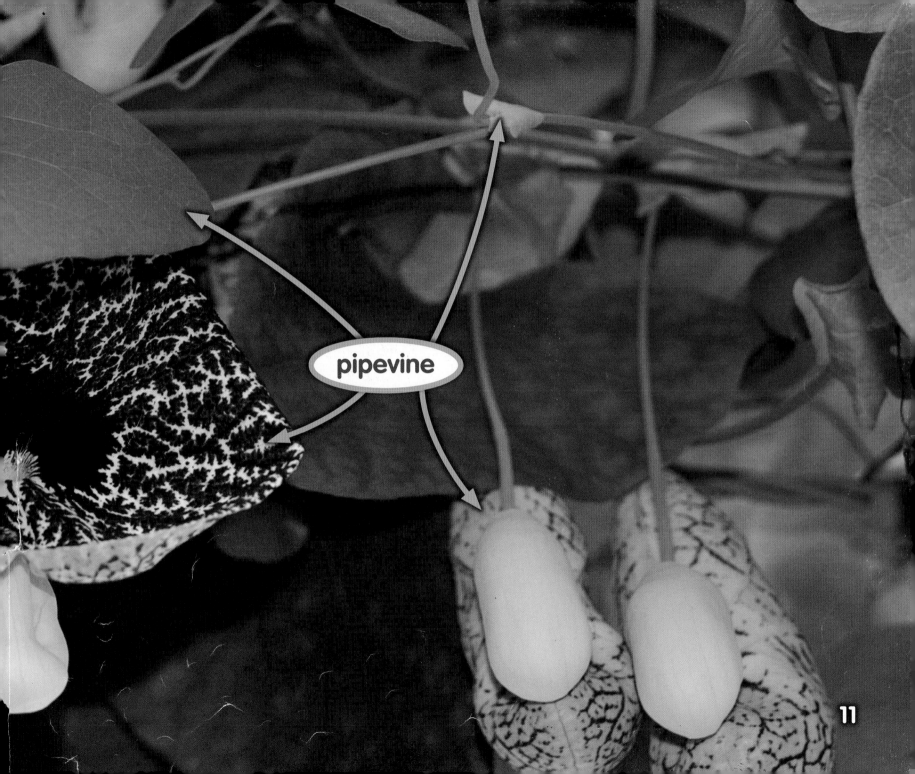

pipevine

Out of the Egg

In eight to ten days, a **caterpillar** comes out of the egg.

The caterpillar's first meal is the egg's hard shell.

Next it eats the leaves of the pipevine.

A female birdwing lays between 30 and 40 eggs in her life. Most butterflies lay more than that.

caterpillar

Eating Poison

The birdwing caterpillar eats only the pipevine.

The plant is harmful to most animals.

Yet birdwing caterpillars can eat the leaves safely.

toad

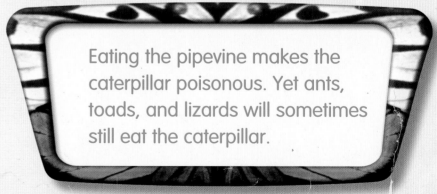

Eating the pipevine makes the caterpillar poisonous. Yet ants, toads, and lizards will sometimes still eat the caterpillar.

Getting Bigger

The Queen Alexandra's birdwing caterpillar eats and eats.

When the caterpillar has grown big enough, it hides under a leaf.

It makes a hard, leathery case for itself.

Inside its case, the caterpillar slowly changes into a butterfly.

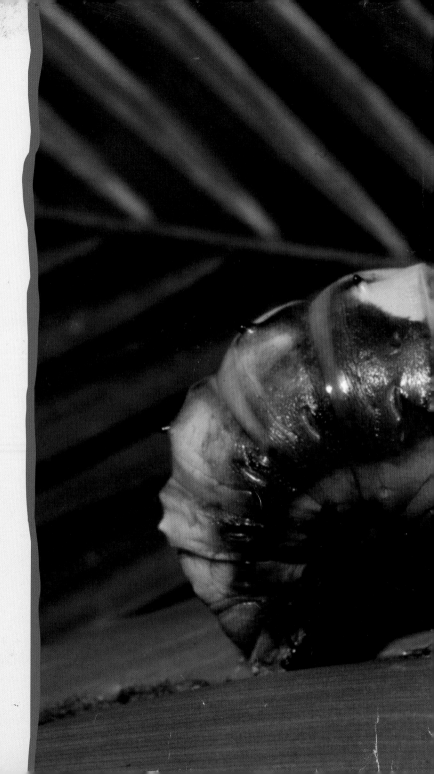

case

The birdwing caterpillar does not eat or move while it is inside its case.

Sipping Food

After about six weeks, a big butterfly comes out of its case.

Like other butterflies, the Queen Alexandra's birdwing sips its food.

Its mouth forms a long tube to drink **nectar** from flowers.

The Queen Alexandra's birdwing can live for three months once it becomes a butterfly.

butterfly coming out of case

Helping the Butterflies

Queen Alexandra's birdwings are in danger.

There are not enough plants for them to eat and lay their eggs on.

In Papua New Guinea, people are growing more plants for the birdwings.

Soon there will be more of these big butterflies flying around the forest!

Queen Alexandra's birdwings are strong and fast flyers.

More Large Insects

Queen Alexandra's birdwings belong to a group of animals called insects. All insects have six legs and a body that is divided into three parts. Most insects hatch from eggs. Though almost all insects have wings, some do not.

Here are three more large insects that fly.

Goliath Birdwing

The Goliath birdwing is the second largest butterfly in the world. Its wings can be 11 inches (28 cm) across.

Giant Swallowtail

The giant swallowtail is the largest butterfly in North America. Its wings can be 6 inches (15 cm) across.

Monarch Butterfly

The monarch butterfly flies long distances. Its wings can be 4.8 inches (12 cm) across.

Queen Alexandra's Birdwing:
12 inches/30 cm

Goliath Birdwing:
11 inches/28 cm

Giant Swallowtail:
6 inches/15 cm

Monarch Butterfly:
4.8 inches/12 cm

Glossary

caterpillar
(KAT-ur-pil-ur)
a wormlike insect that hatches from an egg and changes into a butterfly or moth

pipevine
(PIPE-vine)
a long-stemmed plant that winds around trees and on which the birdwing butterfly lays her eggs

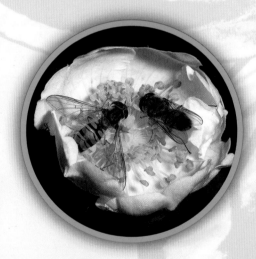

nectar (NEK-tur)
a sweet liquid made by flowers and eaten by insects such as bees and Queen Alexandra's birdwings

rain forests
(RAYN FOR-ists)
large areas of land covered with trees and plants, where lots of rain falls

23

Index

Read More

Ashley, Susan. *Butterflies.* Milwaukee, WI: Gareth Stevens Publishing (2004).

Ehlert, Lois. *Waiting for Wings.* New York: Harcourt Children's Books (2001).

Neye, Emily. *Butterflies.* New York: Penguin Young Readers Group (2000).

Learn More Online

To learn more about Queen Alexandra's birdwings, visit

www.bearportpublishing.com/SuperSized